Idylls from The Garden of Spiritual Delights & Healing

Books by Cheryl Lafferty Eckl

Personal Growth & Transformation

A Beautiful Death:
Keeping the Promise of Love

A Beautiful Grief:
Reflections on Letting Go

The LIGHT Process:
Living on the Razor's Edge of Change

Wise Inner Counselor Books
Reflections on Being Your True Self in Any Situation
Reflections on Doing Your Great Work in Any Occupation
Reflections on Ineffable Love: from loss through grief to joy

Poetry for Inspiration & Beauty

Poetics of Soul & Fire

Bridge to the Otherworld

Idylls from the Garden of Spiritual Delights & Healing

Sparks of Celtic Mystery:
soul poems from Éire

A Beautiful Joy: Reunion with the Beloved
Through Transfiguring Love

Twin Flames Romance Novels

The Weaving:
A Novel of Twin Flames Through Time

Twin Flames of Éire Trilogy
The Ancients and The Call
The Water and The Flame
The Mystics and The Mystery

Idylls from The Garden of Spiritual Delights & Healing

Cheryl Lafferty Eckl

FLYING CRANE PRESS

IDYLLS FROM THE GARDEN OF
SPIRITUAL DELIGHTS & HEALING
© 2016, 2021, 2022 by Cheryl J. Eckl, LLC

Published by Flying Crane Press, Livingston, Montana 59047
Cheryl@CherylEckl.com | www.CherylEckl.com

All rights reserved. No part of this book may be used, reproduced, translated, electronically stored, or transmitted in any manner whatsoever without prior written permission from the author or publisher, except by reviewers, who may quote brief text-only passages in their reviews.

Library of Congress Control Number: 2016903340
ISBN: 978-0-9970376-2-3 (paperback)
ISBN: 978-0-9970376-3-0 (e-book)

Printed in the United States of America

*To all who yearn
for Home*

*Slip in where Mystery dwells:
to your soul's secret Home,
that quiet place of deep communion
where only gentle feet may enter.*

Tender Comfort from the Garden

Spirit delights that you have senses—
portals to receive its wisdom
in the Garden's unhurried affection.

Taste the present moment.

Feel your feet on ancient stones
cool and rippled
or touching green grass—soft and dewy.

Hear the fountain splashing,
singing songs of many waters.

See how wind expands the circle of perception
bending trees, clearing sky of clouds
that disappear over vast grasslands
in the distance.

Breathe in the scent of harmony
from full-bloomed roses on the Garden wall.

And feel the heartbeat of Mother Earth
who enfolds you in her warm embrace
offering tender comfort from her Home—
the world you secretly entered for healing.

Contents

Tender Comfort from the Garden. viii

Enter the Sanctuary of the Heart

    Metamorphosis 3
    The Snow Angel's Gift 4
    Returning to a Familiar Place. 6
    The Green Man's Greeting. 8
    Gaia's Request 12
    The Healing Fountain 18
    Wayfarer's Resolve 21

Taste the Present Moment

    Seraphic Companions 25
    Meeting My Guide 29
    Ah-Lahn's Assurance 32
    The Fairy Ball 34
    Tasting a Warm Breeze 38
    Spirit Sparks. 40

Hear the Songs of Many Waters

    The Sounding Point. 47
    Undine Encounters 48
    Song of My Soul 52
    Seaside Sensations 54
    Many Waters, Many Blessings 56

Breathe in the Scent of Harmony

The Rose Deva's Message 65
A Comforting Perfume 68
Mother of the World 70
Soft. 73
Dolphin Medicine 76
Balancing 80
At Peace Amongst the Pines 81

Expand the Circle of Perception

Symphony of Light and Shadow 85
In the Velvet 86
Power Meets Power 89
Eagle Views 91
A Sylphic Serenade 96
The Ascent 102
Garden Traces 106

Feel the Heartbeat of Mother Earth

Gentle Steps 111
The Grand 112
Communion 114
Bright as Diamonds, Pure as Gold 117
Enough 126

Fly into the Arms of Reunion
Gaia's Blessing 131
The Green Man's Comfort 132
Reunion. 135
Opening the Gift 137
When Two Become One. 141

ILLUSTRATIONS

Madonna of the Lilies (detail) vi
Alphonse Maria Mucha, 1905

Look to the Blowing Rose, Edmund Dulac, 1909 ix

Sir Galahad xiv
George Frederick Watt, 1817-1904

The Moon, Alphonse Maria Mucha, 1902 22

Ophelia, John William Waterhouse, 1910 44

Choosing, George Frederick Watt, 1817-1904 62

Study for Poetry, Alphonse Maria Mucha, 1899 82

Night's Rest, Alphonse Maria Mucha, 1899 108

Two Flying Lovers (Source unknown) 128

Quatrain LXXIII, Rubáiyát of Omar Khayyám 143
René Bull, 1913

Enter the Sanctuary of the Heart

*By the heart
of tender compassion
all life is nourished
to grow again.*

Metamorphosis

Wayfarer, you have made a courageous choice
To cross the bridge to the Unknown—
To show yourself willing to step
Upon this path of mystery.

For many cycles have gone before
Leaving you weary or battle-scarred,
Perhaps wary of what lies beyond
Even when glad companions assert:
Your struggles will be honored here.

How could you anticipate?
This sojourn weaves a cosmic tale
Of Life's eternal unity
That leads to metamorphosis
For those who embrace its healing way.

Our generous Garden welcomes you,
No matter the path you've walked till now.
And luminous beings offer comfort
In peaceful respite from life's toil.

Follow the inspiration that brought you here.
It will keep you single-eyed
Until your journey through this realm
Transforms you from a chrysalis
Into a being with radiant wings
Fashioned out of gratitude
And renewed faith in Nature's art.

The Snow Angel's Gift

As I cross over the silvery bridge
A fairy girl springs into sight
Beaming at me with a smile
Holding a present gaily wrapped
In red foil paper and bright green bow.

Her dress is ballerina length
Made of iridescent cloth
That glistens like finely spun ice—
Her wings as sheer as morning frost
Yet strong enough to carry her
Aloft in a mere instant.

"Hello, Snow Angel," I call to her,
Which makes her laugh at my mistake
Because the Garden is too warm
For winter's chill to enter here.

She twirls around to make it plain
Her garment is ethereal—
And then in merry innocence
She curtseys and holds out her package.

> "This is for you, dear friend,
> Don't open it until you've spent
> More time in Spirit's healing place.

"Until you know the gift is there
Because till then the box will be
Quite empty and of no real use.

Carry it where e're you go
And soon you will discover here
The treasure you had once lost
And are destined to find again—
The gift you're meant to give yourself
And to the world that waits for you."

I take the package from her hands
And feel a tingle up my arms
While clearly stunned to find the box
As light as newborn baby's breath
Yet weighty as a promise made
That strongly calls to be fulfilled.

"See you on the other side!"

She calls out with a gracious wave
Singing while she skips away
In crystalline showers of starlight
That leave a path for me to follow
Into the Garden I have longed to find.

Returning to a Familiar Place

As I near the Garden's gate
A gentle voice whispers to me:

> "You used to live here long ago
> And far away, or so it seems—
> A memory long past and dim
> Faded like an old tintype
>
> With images of other lives,
> Misty thoughts of wisdom lost
> Or perhaps just put away
> Until you could return once more
> After crossing many leagues
> Toward the goal of your Real Self.
>
> It's true that breaking open can
> Bring blessing and a fresh new start
> But only if you sow green seeds
> In fertile ground that life has tilled
>
> Through loss and sudden letting go,
> Or loneliness that rumbles in
> The deepest caverns of the heart
>
> Where sorrow says, 'It is too late.'
> But Hope declares, 'We've just begun!'"

Prompted now to venture forth,
I feel a warmth I've known before—
I hear a sound like spring birdsong
While scent of jasmine, rose, and pine
Waft through the air, lifting my heart
As I feel a tender Presence
That speaks again to my whole being:

> "We welcome your return, brave soul.
> Your trek has brought you here by grace
> And your desire to come back Home
>
> Your stalwart effort to commune
> With Spirit's gifts that are your own
> Even in the darkest hours
> Of deep despair one must traverse
> To reach the Garden of the Heart.
>
> Have faith, dear one, for it is clear
> The seeds you've planted
> Will bear fruit."

I know this now as Gaia's voice—
She who is our Mother Earth
Urging me to enter in
And find solace in her Garden retreat
Of spiritual delights and healing.

The Green Man's Greeting

Breathtaking!
My spontaneous response
To the magnificent silver-haired being
Who greets me at the Garden gate.

This is no jolly, flower-bed gnome
But a sylvan master—emperor-like,
Clad in a suit of mossy green
With diamonds glistening on his lapels
And stardust woven like filigree
Into the fabric of his cape
That spreads behind him billowing
More like a canopy than a cloak.

    "Welcome, dear friend!"

He intones in a voice like velvet thunder,
Powerful, yet silken soft
As eider down or willow tops;
And with a courtly bow informs:

    "I am Gaia's loyal consort
      Sent to say she welcomes you
      As your arrival was foretold."

His form has blocked my view till now,
But as he grandly steps aside
A path of marigolds and fern

Materializes before my eyes
Leading to a plane as vast
As the whole universe itself,
Yet as intimate as the simple abode
That is my cozy earth-time home.

Celestial music fills the air
As flowers, grasses, vines, and trees
All sing a wordless melody
That feels like balm unto my soul
And ceaseless joy that fills my heart.

"Is this heaven or a dream?"
 I ask my host in amazement.

　　"Some have called it Paradise."

His eyes are twinkling as he bids
Me sit beside a splashing pool
Whose waters dance, seemingly alive
With fishes, dolphins, and sea nymphs.
Then he assures me with gracious ease:

　　"Oh, Gaia's Garden is very real.
　　 It is meant to illuminate,
　　　Protect and guide you to your goal.
　　　Now, please accept some refreshment."

He offers me a brimming cup
Of effervescent crystal liquid
Whose bubbles tingle on my tongue
And spark a flash electrical
That *whooshes!* down into my toes
Then back from the ground up to my head
Kindling a wakefulness sublime.

He smiles at my astonishment,
And then proceeds to instruct me
About the purpose of my sojourn
In this place that has been closed
To earthly eyes for centuries:

> "Embrace all you witness here.
> And then recite the story well
> Of what harmony can manifest
>
> When all of life cooperates
> In mutual kindness and respect
> For each one's place in a web of life
> As Spirit's Presence first conceived.
>
> We offer you an extended tour—
> A bit like your *Arabian Nights*
> To witness and become entwined
> With land and sea and sky above

"And all living things abiding here
That you might comprehend anew
Creation's finest handiwork.

We beg you tell the tales of wonder
And transformation one finds here
That other wayfarers may be inspired
To seek the Garden on their own

So we might raise up consciousness
And hope of healing in the psyches
We long to welcome through these gates.

Mercy bids you stay awhile
To learn the secrets of this place,
The Eden held in Gaia's heart—
May it become your *Home, Sweet Home.*"

Gaia's Request

The Garden is a friendly place—
A warm oasis of well-being
Strong, yet gentle and supportive
As if the entire atmosphere
Were charged with tender loving-kindness
And intimate knowledge of my soul.

Into this blissful, verdant setting
Gracefully steps the Mother Gaia,
Clothed in finest gauzy robes
Like layer upon layer of wedding veils
With crimson roses and camellias
Sewn into the airy fabric.

Vines stream cape-like from her shoulders
Lilies crown her auburn tresses
And in her hand a staff of office
Glowing like a rod of power.

She is aware of my deep longing
For this encounter, and so greets me
With open arms and warmest smile
That reassure my eager heart
As I tearfully embrace her.

Gently linking her arm in mine
She beckons me to walk with her
Into a grove of apple trees

Where we may converse quietly,
While in the cheerful company
Of rabbits, eagles, foxes, and sparrows
Who gather in her shimmering aura.

Seated in a gilded chair
She waits for me to settle down
My mind and wildly beating heart,
So I may receive her discourse:

An urgent message for her children
That will speak of Garden secrets
To be shared as collaboration
Between the unseen and the seen.

Once I am still, she begins to speak
Her voice a melody of grace:

> "Beloved one, be you at peace
> As are all creatures gathered here."

Sweeping her arm in a grand gesture
She reveals animals of every kind
Plus radiant beings from spirit realms—
An endless array of presences
Who seem as one great teeming body
Alive with cosmic consciousness.

Gaia's Message:
"You see we are united here
In purest harmony and honor
Of each one's special role and gift
Essential to all others' place
In Life's great web of which you are
A much beloved part, my dear.

This Garden is the Otherworld
The Place Beyond, where you have longed
To come for counsel, growth, and healing
Between past lives and in your dreams.

It has been closed to daytime minds,
But earthly challenges demand
The veil be lifted for human eyes,
So you might see with waken'd sight
The secrets of an inner path
That leads to freedom for all life.

You bring with you a mighty gift
As yet unopened to your mind
To be discovered as you explore
The depth and breadth of this magical place

And the earthly one it joins
To teach you about unity
With myriad aspects of our planes.

"Consider your mission a treasure hunt
A journey into Mystery
For which I offer you a clue:

> *Whether sleeping or awake*
> *The Garden you traverse is real.*
> *Even landscape has consciousness*
> *And you are every being you'll meet.*

Guides will lead your travels here
Sent by me and many others
So you might learn of Spirit's ways
And share them with those who long
To find their way back Home for good.

This pilgrimage is meant to be
A conversation between worlds
That you'll experience on many levels
As you dance upon the bridge
Connecting supernal realms with Earth.

Follow your guide who knows these planes
As intimately as he knows your heart.
Listen well both day and night
Attend with all your finest senses
And carry back the Garden's essence
Of celestial hospitality
That offers hope and unity.

"Let this Garden be for you
A sanctuary of the heart
Where you will learn of mystic truths
Of soul delights and transformation
So you might be a force of healing
From the ethers to the land.

For though you only visit now
We count you as a traveler
Who will return before too long."

Bestowing, then, upon my cheek
A kiss as light as a fairy's wing
She causes a shower of lilies
To rain upon me as I stand

Amazed, ecstatic, overwhelmed
By her effulgent loveliness
And my own tears of gratitude
That I should witness such a being
And that she should make request of me.

As she disappears into the mist
I shake my head—*Is this a dream?*
Then reaching out, I touch the box—
The Snow Angel's package at my side.

Lifting it up, I feel its weight
A slight increase inside the gift
As if a fragment had been added—
An intriguing start, to be sure.

It's Gaia's clue!
Now I understand—
I need not look inside the box
To confirm that her request
Is safely anchored in my mind:

> *That I should sojourn as she desires*
> *Open to experiences*
> *With sentient creatures*
> *And landscapes.*

And as I muse upon my task,
I find myself ushered along
By an insistent bunny rabbit
Who aims me toward a hidden grotto
Then hops away without a sound.

So I walk on in faith and hope
To my next magical encounter
That I pray will bring me insight
And surcease from earthly toil.

The Healing Fountain

Near the entrance to the Garden
is an unassuming fountain
half hidden by a latticed wall
of jasmine, vines, and honeysuckle—
simple in its classical design
yet vast in scope for those who know
it can contain a universe
of healing waters in its pool.

After enduring challenging lives,
souls come here to be relieved
of burdens that can be transmuted
in the dynamic cleansing power
of liquid light that leaps to greet them
as they begin their next transition.

Some experience a shower
descending like myriad sunbeams
while others plunge into
a bath of pearl-like purity,
and all feel sublimely infused
with its mercy that prepares them
for the Garden's transformative grace.

As I approach it springs to life
with airy sprays that spin and sway
like angels dancing on a silver disc
that expands wider and wider

until I am fully enveloped
in sheets of misty diamond radiance
that is conscious of itself
and of our interaction—
playful, joyous, and determined
that every aspect of my being
should be revived and enlightened.

Suddenly the light starts whirling,
all the sprays combined as one
in a gigantic spinning spiral
like a cylinder of rainbows

luminous with shooting white rays
creating exquisite iridescence
and a sound of purest tone
as if a vibrant symphony
of crystal singing bowls
were being played by angel hands.

And then just as suddenly
the whirling stops as all goes still—
the fountain once more
a calm blue pool,
and I am standing at a distance
feeling like myself again
though not at all as how I was,
for something has been taken away.

I sit and ponder what is new—
a finer curiosity, that's sure,
to know more of the Garden's depth
with insight so I'll understand
the treasures I'm allowed to see.

But now I feel a vacancy
where certain types of fear once lodged,
and meditating now I know:

*The fountain took my reticence
to quest for visions on this journey
that embraces Spirit's Light.*

A sense of worthiness has come
to take the place of my resistance
so I may sojourn with courage
ready to receive what's given.

Wayfarer's Resolve

Vigor is asked of those
    who desire to walk in the Garden
    as participants in its mysteries

    who long to connect with its inhabitants
    becoming one with trees and grasses
    even scrubs and mossy lichens.

All beings play their roles with passion
    in this idyllic web of life,
    reaching for the sun
    that calls them to itself

    each embracing each in mutual delight
    and profound camaraderie of sharing
    adventures in this dimension.

Is it possible to so intimately resonate
    with Gaia's vibrant song
    that one may hear it
    caroling through the pure air

    loving her world into being
    again and again and again?

Trusting it is so,
    I take a deep breath
    and set my gaze toward the horizon.

Taste the Present Moment

*Poems feel like letters from the gods
and taste like ambrosia
on the tongue that speaks them.*

Seraphic Companions

As a full moon rises
Bathing the landscape
In swaths of silver radiance
Legions of incandescent seraphim
Appear as rings upon rings
Of ethereal presences

Filling the heavens with their luminosity,
The brilliance of their intelligence,
Their adoration of Spirit
Wherever it may manifest.

O, how thrilling to witness this scene!
In earthly planes they are hidden from view
Though I have felt them as a child
And as an adult in crisis times.
When life seemed all too much to bear
I somehow knew I was not alone.

Here in the Garden they are quite apparent.
So I reach out now and gently touch
The resplendent one right by my side
Who has been ever-present for my sake

Who has carried me through thick and thin
Even when I lost my faith,
And now clearly rejoices that I've come
To this place where seraphs abide.

The Seraph Speaks:
"O, precious soul, who are my own,
My caring for you knows no bounds—
For your celestial guard am I
Ever present in life and death
Always watchful as you travel.

For your safe passage through life
Is my eternal priority—
That you should never suffer fear
But rather feel our holy Love
In the touch of angel wings
And comfort during the challenges
That must come to all wayfarers.

And now I wish to share with you
A secret about seraphim
That you might understand our role
In the unfolding of your life.

Though you meet us singly
We seraphim serve in pairs
Who alternate in a cosmic dance
That takes us to celestial realms
Then back again to tend your soul.

One seraph gazes at the sun
Taking in its brilliant rays

"Recharging for the work to come,
While the other cares for you
In the service that we cherish
To keep you always safe from harm.

Then once a cycle do we turn
To face each other in unity
And recognition of our bond
As we take up our partner's task
In unconditional devotion
To each other and to you.

We seraphs live in the eternal *now*
And in our timeless vigilance
We relish every moment with you
Especially here where you see us.

O, how we long to work with you
In a conscious partnership
To be invited to participate
In creating a life of perfect flow.

For seraphim don't interfere
In the free will of human kind.
It is the highest law of being
That we obey most faithfully.

"We take pleasure in your happiness
And always do we celebrate
Attending merry festivals

Rejoicing in your victories
When you have kept Love's promises
That lead you to your own True Self.

For we have surely guarded you
From life to life and perhaps beyond—
To far-flung worlds or galaxies
And garden realms such as this one.

Even here in Gaia's home
We watch over those who come and go
Arranging reunions for beloveds
Who desire to meet again
After living separate lives.

And so, my dearest, precious one,
Sojourn in faith upon this path,
For you will never be alone
Where e're you go in time and space
Or here in this timeless realm.

We are always at your side
Whether you see us here or not.
Call to us in times of need
We are your own loyal seraphim."

Meeting My Guide

He appears to be the gardener
Sitting casually on a bench
Resting from his many labors,
Perhaps reflecting on future tasks
Or simply relishing the flowers
That have blossomed in his care.

Looking up, his gaze meets mine,
And I thrill to see the face,
The sea-green eyes and sculptured jaw
Of the one I prayed was here—

The truest advocate of my soul
Whose love has called me to this place
That we might be again together,
If even for a little while.

"Come and sit beside me, dear."

He says, as a rosy sphere of Light
Emanates out from his heart
Enveloping the two of us.

He takes my hands into his own,
Peers into my eyes with affection
So deep that it melts straight away
All vestiges of doubt or fear.
Then he speaks again most tenderly:

"I've been waiting for you here,
Though not so long as you might think
For time is nothing on this plane
And I am patient, as you know.

Plus, I could see you on the bridge
Doing your best to find your way
Into Mother Gaia's realm.

That you have come this far today
Counts toward our mutual boon
For which you have my gratitude."

And then he smiles down at the tears
That well up in my eyes and throat
So I can barely speak the words:

I've tried so hard to come to you.

For now I know him as Ah-Lahn,
The faithful guide who loves me most
Who has forever tended my soul
Often out of human sight

Yet ever present in my heart
And sometimes even by my side
As he acknowledges and says:

"I know, dear one.
Now that you're here
Our work together begins anew
As hand in hand we can fulfill
Gaia's request and so much more.

You, who have the gift of words,
Take up your journal and your pen,
You'll need no other implements
Except your open mind and heart

And your firm will to convey
The mysteries I transfer to you
For the sake of your own soul
And for those who long to know
The Garden's essence and the flame
Of what it means to enter here.

Come with me now,
We're on our way
To explore this Place Beyond—
The destiny you have long sought,
You, who are my own sweet love."

Ah-Lahn's Assurance

Should you ever doubt your path
In a momentary weakness,
Depend upon your Garden guide
To speak into your wavering thoughts
Words of comfort and support
As Ah-Lahn now offers me:

> "I say that you are worthy, dear—
> And not merely for merit earned
> Through your effort and devotion,
> But for grace and for the sake
> Of those whose lives you're meant to touch.
>
> Worth is of the seasoned heart
> That embraces Love's challenges,
> Receives its sweetness when offered,
> And cares enough to let it go
> When, sadly, others pull away.
>
> Doubt can sully worthiness
> And spoil the gift of partnership
> We long to share with those we meet
> In this brilliant Otherworld
> That is your own soul's destiny.
>
> Here in the Garden we persevere
> To run this race to its completion
> As heroes and heroines have always done.

"Fear not, beloved, you've allies aplenty
And a universe of helpers
Resting in glad anticipation
That you will tell their favorite stories
When you return to earthly climes.

I will not desert you, no matter what—
Be you in or out of heavenly spheres.
Stay open to me where e'er you go
And trust our mutual intuition
For I have lessons to impart
To raise us both to higher realms."

The Fairy Ball

Do fairies dance for more than fun?
Is there a larger purpose found
In the rituals of gnomes and elves
Who frolic in the clear moonlight,
Creating circles in the grass
Or gilding lilies with their charms?

The answer comes from a sylvan elf
Resting high in a grand oak tree:

> "Why yes, the Garden operates
> In perpetual three-quarter time
> Transforming burdens into bliss
> For those who come here to be healed.
>
> Nature's true being reaches out
> To partner in co-creation's work.
> Even the tiniest creatures strive
> To bond their hearts in unity
> That each one may give of their gifts
> In balance and in harmony."

This elegant fellow wears a tux and tails
As if he were going to a formal ball.

> "Oh, I am," he reads my mind.
> "You should come too, for everyone
> You'll want to meet will be on hand.
> A visit here is not complete
> Until you've danced at the Fairy Ball."

I follow my host to a tree-lined glen
An expansive gathering place
All aglow with twinkling lights
Where dancing music fills the air
Played on fiddles, pipes, and drums
By a sprightly elf ensemble.

While all the Garden residents
Adorned in their resplendent best—
Brilliant feathers, shiny fur
And iridescent gossamer wings,
Waltz round and round in gaiety
Creating spirals of rainbow Light
That flow out as healing rays.

The scene is irresistible.
Even flower devas dance,
Drawing me in to join the fun
With fairy beings, gnomes, and elves.
O, how my heart soars up in wonder!

Amidst this balletic jubilee
I feel a firm tug on my sleeve.
It is my elfin counterpart
Urging me to a secluded place
Where a transparent gazebo stands
Shimmering with a cozy glow
Reminding me of homes I've known.

He bows and says most graciously:

> "We've planned a special treat for you.
> Some of your friends have come tonight
> And want to greet you privately."

Intrigued and hopeful, I step inside
A gorgeous room of crystalline glass
Seeing at first only clustered lights
Whose facial features then grow clear
As my heart bursts open in surprise.

For gathered here are my best friends,
The dearest I have known of yore
Even some from this lifetime
Exuding childlike playfulness
Unburdened as they seem to be—
Radiating jewel-like hues
Each one unique, yet familiar.

One who glistens light blue and gold
Comes up first to welcome me:

> "We're so grateful you've arrived
> To share the Fairy Ball with us.
> We never miss the fun or food.
>
> Please try this violet-flower sorbet.
> It is our favorite ambrosial delight—
> Rightfully esteemed as food for gods.

"Of course, we are curious to learn
About your adventures in this realm.
Did Snow Angel give you a wrapped box?
Have you met Gaia and your guide?

But first, let's dance and play the game
Of tossing purple spheres around.
Our group all like this one the best
To enhance our vibrancy
While basking in the Garden's glow."

O, what a glorious exchange!
Of deep kinship and secret lore
That all made sense according to
Each friend's gifts and history.

Affection reigned in every heart.
'Twas borne of mutual promises
To help each other on the path
We've shared since human time began
So each of us may grow more wise
And gain in soul reality.

Do fairies dance for more than fun?
I cannot help but feel they do.
Their felicity most certainly creates
An atmosphere where dear friends meet
As mine did at the Fairy Ball.

Tasting a Warm Breeze

Here again
just as before—
when I began to emerge
from dusky climes,
re-birthed to living
a new way
as a different person—
or better said,
as transformed
into a truer self

a warm breeze
is blowing through my soul
into my form,
ever so gently
enveloping the tender places,
spiraling around
in my chest,
radiating out
like an inner angel
spreading her soft wings.

If eyes are soul windows,
mine are widening open
to receive delicate impressions
of stars and moon beams,
intimations of loveliness,
deep knowings that only souls can tell.

A new day is dawning
fresh and pure
as if from long ago
before the world was.

These are hours of exultation
felt within and without
as Spirit's Garden is revealed.

Elysian fields were never
so bright with greens
and purples, ruby, gold,
cerulean blue

all held together
by a rose of peace
watered by the dew
of heaven's laughter

tasting of Life's
sweet, warm breeze
that caresses my cheek
like fairy kisses.

Spirit Sparks

One disappointment of my trek thus far
Has been not meeting fiery salamanders.
I've heard they emit pure delight
And no one has more fun than they.

An elf explains their reticence
To join in fairy balls and such:

> "You see, we've had some problems here
> With salamander exuberance.
> They get so excited at large parties
> That they have a tendency
> To set the decorations on fire
> As well as the occasional guest.
>
> If you desire their company
> Journey to the Garden's center
> Where there burns a perpetual flame
> Surrounded by these elementals
> Whom we all honor for their work."

My spirits are high as I hurry along
Arriving at what turns out to be
A giant blaze of brilliant colors—
Centered on a ruby flame
Which is the hue of Divine Love.
And all around it myriad sparks
Like living candles, dancing and diving

In and out of the rainbow blaze
Whirling and swirling with jubilation
That makes my heart leap up to say:
I know these beings like my own name!

"My darling friends! O, how I've missed you!"
I cry out in spite of myself.

They suddenly stop and turn around,
Then here they flash in a great swarm
Surrounding me like fireflies.

"We knew you'd come!
We just *knew* it!

We've watched you since you were a child
Spending hours by the hearth
Gazing into fireplace fires
Your father taught you how to build.

Did you feel our presence then?
Could you see us smiling back?

Did you know that those hearth flames
Sent our vibration to your soul
To sustain you through trials and hurts
Until you could come visit here
To join in our flamboyant play.

"Precious one, dreams do come true,
   The fun you've sought begins right now."

Before I can answer, their flames flare up
My heart expands into a furnace
Enveloping my entire being
So I am now as one of them.

Exuberantly we leap together
Into the opalescent fire
That burns and yet does not consume
Itself or me or my fiery friends.

Somehow this blaze does not feel hot
Yet here we are, right in its midst.
We are in fact, all made of flame
Whirling 'round in radiant spirals
Spinning faster than light speed.

And now we all begin to chant—
Singing as we carry on
Kindled with euphoria:

>   *Burn, O Home fires! Blaze up bright!*
>   *We are the keepers of the flame*
>   *Of the Garden's soul center—*
>   *The living zeal of Mother Gaia.*

We are the flame, we are the fire
The source of Life—we never tire.
We are the beginning and the end
We warm your hearts, eternal friends.

Count on us for spirit sparks
Whenever life becomes too hard.
We transform darkness into Light.

We bring compassion to the night
Of mankind's woes and sufferings
We dissolve them all with our hearth song.

We are the fire, we are the flame
Call to us in Freedom's name
And we will make your souls burn bright
With good will and pure delight.

Truly, this is my childhood dream
To be the flame, not merely gaze
To feel the warmth of ruby fire
To be imbued with inspiration
Then sent forth on my path alight—

A spirit spark of fiery Love.
To carry on in my own heart.

Hear the Songs of Many Waters

*Dive deep into this reality
and swim in the lake
of soul comfort and truth.*

The Sounding Point

While watching me
from her tidal pool,
a little sea nymph suggests
how to listen in the Garden:

"Rest here till you feel
the tears of soul recognition
signaling that you
have made contact
with another being's essence.

Still yourself
and let the frontier
come to you
speaking of Eternity

as the great blue whales
carry records of a time
when our two worlds were one.

Once you feel the tenderness
of your feet in salty water,
you will begin
to know your heart
as the sounding point of unity

that speaks the language of the soul
and calls you to a larger life
of endless possibility."

Undine Encounters

Seeking a place to rest a while
I sit down beside a cool green lake
Serene in its perfect stillness
That invites me to settle into
The reverie and peaceful calm
Its waters engender in this place.

Here my soul breathes in
The Garden's heavenly atmosphere
Next to the glassy surface
That mirrors clouds and rocky crags
Once lifted up from the valley floor
Now speechless in their grandeur.

Suddenly I sense the movement
Of unseen forces congregating
Out in the lake's watery depths
As if spirit beings were gathering
In profound communion,
Whispering secrets my heart longs
To know and can only imagine.

Overcome by curiosity and determined
Not to be left in ignorance,
I surprise myself
By walking into the water
Which feels like silk against my skin
As I slip beneath the surface

To be met by a group of undines
Their long hair flowing around
Lithe bodies, twirling to and fro
In the crystal clear lake waters.

"Did you come to play?"

They ask, giggling and splashing,
Creating air bubbles
That rise to the surface
In rainbow spheres.

"No," I answer, amazed that I am
Breathing under water.

"I'm here to learn about
The spirit council underway
Out there in the lake."

> "Only guides are invited
> To those gatherings,
> And even if you swam close,
> You wouldn't be able to see them.
> But if you stay with us,
> We'll tell you all our secrets."

And then they all laugh again,
Spinning and turning in spirals

Up to the surface
Then down to the lake bottom
Chasing each other in a game of tag
Until they come to a sudden halt,
Saying in impish seriousness:

"Actually, we have only *one* secret!"
Flow!
Flow!
Flow!
Flow!

They repeat the word again and again
In a mellifluous mantra that propels them
Into a sort of water ballet
As their melody goes on this way:

Flow with the water
Flow with the moment
Flow with the music of what's happening
Or of empty time and space.

Flow is how the Garden works
Flow is all you need to know!

Sometimes flow means being okay
With what you are able to know today
And understanding there are realms
Where you are not prepared to go.

Don't worry, just stay in the flow
And tomorrow there will be much more
Of what you are allowed to know.

"Do you like our song?
 We'd sing it again
 But now we need
 To send you back
  Onto dry land for a little while."

And with a happy splash, *Good-bye,*
The undines disappear from view.

Sitting once more at the water's edge
I look out across the glassy lake.

"See you again!"
 I call after my frolicsome friends.
 And laugh until euphoric tears
 Roll down my face.

Song of My Soul

"Sing to me," my love requests,
"A gentle tune of happy hope.
 I used to relish when you sang
 From innocence and simple joy,
 When you forgot self-consciousness
 Letting Spirit take control
 So you merged with the melody."

"I fear those days are long since passed."
 It pains me to admit my voice
 Has slipped away from lack of use.

"Not so!" he cries, "for I am here
 And with me you are Garden-skilled.
 Every creature has its tune,
 Even rocks and flowers sing
 And you who came to life with song
 Will find your special keynote here."

How I hope he tells me true
For music has profoundly moved me
With its power to lift and heal
The lowest of spirits or broken hearts.

"Just sing one note—give it a try!"

My precious guide draws me to my feet
And so I voice a simple *ah*.
But as I sound my single tone

A thousand voices answer me
At least five octaves high to low.

I sing again, a different note,
And all the Garden joins the fun.
A musical repartee ensues—
An antiphon of harmony

As fauna, flora, and spirit beings
Add to the dulcet noise that fills
My heart with ecstasy as if
I were an instrument being played
By the song that rings and thrills
From every realm. *O, such delight!*

A great crescendo now is reached
As enraptured voices soar.
I feel that I might fly away
Till my guide looks into my eyes
With a steady gaze that says:

> "Never doubt me, my dear one,
> For here such miracles abound.
> Absorb this song and carry it
> Always safe in your memory.
>
> This is your soul's own golden tone,
> A sound ray that will bring you here
> Whenever you seek sanctuary."

Seaside Sensations

Garden ocean majesty
bustling with visual artistry
and symphonic thunderings
that capture all my senses
bringing me alive to life
in all of its exhilaration

deep roaring reverberations
of huge swells
crashing on rocks
far out from the shore

sea birds circling overhead
crying in treble voices

sotto voce wave murmurs
of furls and fans
spreading their skirts
in bubble-rimmed flourishes
thin and determined
as a cool tide
comes nipping at my toes

dazzling afternoon sun
blazing its reflection
from sky to waves to beach
overwhelming my eyes
with its brilliance

tangy sea air
most delicious of all
thick with the taste of Eternity

solid-feeling strand
damp beneath my feet

recording impressions
only to see them
washing away
by perpetual tides
rolling in and out
refreshing
the clean, white-sand page

readying it
to be writ upon
once more,
though finding it
undisturbed by sensations
of impermanence

even when this numinous ocean
goes strangely quiet
for an instant

Many Waters, Many Blessings

Out of myth and misty stories
From the Garden's far-flung corners
Come four magnificent beings
Emerging from their deep-water lairs
To tell the truth of their existence
And share a message from their hearts.

Some say they are the *Sluagh Sídhe**
The fairy-folk who gather 'round
Holy springs and river sources,
While others call them water gods
And goddesses of Neptune's realm.

Water dragons are they, in fact,
Both male and female in two pairs
Bathed in light and glistening
With rainbow colors all along
The full extent of their huge bodies
Made of iridescent scales.

Charged are they by Mother Gaia
With the task of regulating
Life-sustaining water's flow
Through streams and lakes and rivers proud
From waterfalls and mighty oceans
In and all around the Garden.

* (pronounced "sloo-ah-shee")

Suddenly they impart as with one voice:

> "We sing the songs of many waters,
> Which you might not anticipate
> As utterances of dragon throats.
> Not all our species are fire breathers
> For us the heat is in our hearts.
> We send forth music from our lips."

Each one sings a unique song
That nourishes and tames the water
Over which they have dominion
Sustained for all Eternity.

The first to reveal his melody
Is a great blue male called *Water Thunder*
His sound—the mighty roar of cascades
Crashing over rocky ramparts
Carving canyons with their power
Filling the air with sparkling ions
Inspiring artists with their grandeur.

His mate, known as *Pacifica*,
Glorious in her turquoise body,
Bears the song of peaceful waters
The gentle tune of lakes and pools
Whose subtle ripples nourish beings
In still, deep places or shallow wetlands.

La Grande Belle Dame du Terre
Is the silver dragon's name
Though they call her *La Mer* for short—
A little joke amongst themselves
For she has the biggest voice,
The widest and most complex range
Of decibel and varied pitch.

> "It takes a female," she explains
>   With perfect confidence and grace,
> "To sing the ocean's symphony."

So she begins in a deep bass tone
Of far-off waves on coral reefs
As great big walls of foamy breakers
Rush to shore like trumpets sounding
Cymbals crashing to diminish at last
On the beach in lacy wavelets
Soft like a harpist's light glissando.

La Mer's mate, called *Laughing Water,*
Shining in more earthy tones,
Nods in honor of her mastery
Amidst his happy burbling song
That speaks of dulcet splashing brooks
And streams that swiftly carve their course,
Rills and rivulets that frolic
Merging into rushing rivers

That surrender at their power's peak
To join *La Mer's* majestic realm.

So the water dragons hold
In the Garden's corner points
The sacred Source from which all life
Springs forth, retaining perfect balance

Through compassion in their hearts
Mercy glistening in their eyes
And on their lips an ancient vow
To never let the music die.

Clearly there is purpose here,
I know this is no accident
That we should congregate together
In such auspicious circumstance.

So I open up my mind
To receive the deeper messages
These mighty dragons would impart
Into my eager consciousness;
For I am feeling profound kinship
With creatures thought to be a myth.

Together, then, they speak again
As one great, resounding voice:

"Unlike Earth's capricious waters
Here we have no floods or storms
To disturb the Garden's wholeness
Or its atmosphere of peace.

Yet so many come for healing
Angel guides could use your help,
For by your prayers are they more able
To assist those with the greatest need.

We ask that you chant and pray
So the Garden flourishes
In the conscious minds of those
Who would enter here for comfort's balm.

By your faithful meditations
Are these waters kept alive
For them as beacons of Spirit's Truth,
Its Goodness and eternal Beauty—
The elements that call souls Home
To find renewal and surcease
From the cares of worldly life.

Our task is to sustain these waters,
Just as yours is to make known
That Earth and Garden work together
Where the veil between worlds thins.

"We are here for your salvation.
Your devotion helps ensure
That all who seek the Garden find it.

So they may commune with us,
Perhaps to join us in our songs
Of many waters, many blessings
That keep their souls both safe and whole."

As fluidly as they had come
The water dragons slip away
Each one to a noble home
Leaving in their sparkling wake
A dewdrop of their consciousness.

I feel as one newly baptized
By a mist of holy water.

Breathe in the Scent of Harmony

*Peace inhabits the receptive mind
made empty of conditions
that would lock the door
to Spirit's deepest knowing.*

The Rose Deva's Message

Garden roses are miraculous
Thorn-less, defenseless, and hospitable,
Luminously fragrant and sparkling
As if kissed by eternal dew

Thriving in flower bed communities
Trailing over trellises and bowers
Bathing great swaths of the Garden
In exquisitely sweet perfumes
Without subduing other flowers.

As I gaze in *sub rosa* reverie
A fairy-like creature—the Rose Deva
Emerges in a gossamer gown
Speaking from a bed of lavender blooms
That Gaia has named *Angel Face*
In honor of their heavenly scent.

> "You know, we're not just pretty faces.
> We live to share our healing essence
> As we have done for millennia
> To soothe the weariest of souls
> Who come to the Garden for respite.
>
> We roses are an ancient breed
> Which gives us leave and the honor
> Of orienting newer buds
> And supporting our flower kin
> On myriad worlds and dimensions
> In many planes of consciousness.

"Roses are faithful to the end
　The first to arrive and the last to leave.
　We do not question our own existence
　Or compete for who blooms best
　We honor each one's special gift
　Of selfless giving unto others
　So souls may ascend to loftier realms.

　If you would understand the Garden
　In deep communion with our Mother
　Inhale the fragrance of the rose
　And learn the secrets of our nature."

I could not wait another moment
To breathe in their redolent scent
Absorbing the unfettered care
Roses are free to emanate here
Where tender petals are quite safe

To feel their constant adoration
Of Spirit that lives in every heart,
As gratitude suddenly floods my soul
For the untold blessings I received
From the hand of my own mother.

Roseate essence heals all wounds
And opens hearts to transmuation
Of burdens we may have placed
Upon the ones who loved us first

So we may forgive each other
And unite as kindred souls.

Thus, as my contemplation deepens
The Rose Deva speaks a message of hope
For all of us who journey Home:

> "Be at peace, my own dear one,
> Allow the flower of your heart
> To open up as Nature guides
> In the warmth of our sure care.
>
> Bloom where you're planted
> And trust the Garden
> To lead you on your soul's journey.
>
> Seek not sensations nor insights
> Beyond what you may grasp today.
> There is time enough to grow
> Here in the realms of timelessness.
>
> We know your deepest soul desires
> For they were placed there by the Mother
> And the Father of us all.
>
> Be true, dear one, and faithful to
> The mission you have sought of old;
> A gift of knowledge is at hand.
>
> Become a sweet, enchanting rose
> And all will be well in no time."

A Comforting Perfume

Leela and Loki are animal guides—
Smart, intuitive shepherd dogs,
Recently graduated to the Garden
After years of loyal service
To their true-blue human friend.
I had wondered if I might find them
And, sure enough, they have found me.

> "We knew you by your scent, of course,
> From the fragrance of your soul.
> Just as a rose has its perfume,
> Every sentient being's essence
> Tickles our noses with their identity.
>
> Your bouquet is one of kindness
> Tangy with your love of dogs.
> Follow now, we've got lots to teach you
> Especially about your sense of smell."

Running up a Garden path
Lined with fragrant lilac bushes
My doggie guides urge me to hurry
And not tarry midst the blooms.

> "Don't dawdle, our time here is short
> We usually focus on your world
> Prompting humans to trust their senses
> As they wend their way through life.

"Make good use of your Garden visit
To improve your sense of smell
In detecting subtleties
Of aromas strong or faint.

Soak up the scents of harmony
That permeate this fragrant air
So when you're in Earth's denser plane
You'll be able to sniff out
Thoughts or feelings, people or things
That do not savor as they should
If you intend to bring them home.

Your nose can be like a guide dog—
Follow it as shepherds do
To points of warmth and nourishment,
Affection borne in caring hearts
Who only want the best for you."

With that advice, they bound away
Back to their work with human friends
Who need their loyalty and guidance
In the ways of dog wisdom.

And as they leave, I note the scent
That is for me a comforting perfume
Of sweet dog kisses and puppy breath—
For in the Garden are all made new.

Mother of the World

Seated on a rock outcropping
Shaped like a giant lotus flower
Mother Gaia meditates,
Emanating from her aura
An energetic invitation
To all of us who long to merge
With the waves of the Infinite.

She rests upon a divan of pillows
Richly woven in purple hues,
Her mantle an intricate tapestry
With images of mythic creatures
Embroidered in shimmering golden threads
Upon field of silvery blue.

My soul group and I congregate
With visitors and residents,
Waiting for—I know not what,
Only that my heart is burning
With fervent anticipation.

Mother Gaia asks for silence
And intones the sacred *AUM*
That reverberates around the Garden
Quivering the ethers just as if
A thousand conch shells were being sounded
Calling all sentient beings Home.

Our glad assembly joins her chanting
In perfect choral harmony
While the tone resounds unceasingly
Now echoing about the landscape,
As though the ground and sea and sky
Might possess voices that can sing
In response to this great being's
Sending *AUM* throughout the Garden
As Eternity's seed sound.

Our communion now grows deeper
Into Mother Gaia's service.
I feel her voice within my body
Penetrating to my heart
With her compassionate intention:

Breathe me, dear one, while I breathe thee.

United are we in her aura
So all together we now exhale,
Emptying ourselves of resistance
To Mother Gaia's Presence with us.

As she breathes in I feel as if
She's taking my pulse or the measure
Of every creature gathered here
Absorbing each distinctive fragrance
To determine what we need.

While her inhalation lengthens
I feel a tug on my own breath
Encouraging release of what I am holding.
And as I let go with all the others
A cloud of darkness manifests
Wafting swiftly toward Mother Gaia
Nearly obscuring her from view

Until she completely breathes it in
All the way into her heart
Which instantly grows incandescent—
An enormous furnace of transforming radiance
Consuming every bit of substance
Until the atmosphere around her
Glows in rings of glistening Light.

Only then does she exhale
A vibrant breath of sublime sweetness
Scented of violets and gardenias—
A heady perfume of transmutation
Flowing into our open hearts

Which now breathe back to Mother Gaia
In communion with our spirits,
Each one drinking in the other
Then exhaling Light and Love,
Until she nods in gracious conclusion,
Sending forth a final *AUM*.

Soft

An aromatic serenity
envelopes the idyllic scene
as a soft breeze murmurs
through honeysuckle vines
wafting their ambrosial fragrance
to my grateful heart,
ruffling tree tops
and sending seedlings
dancing off
to find new beds for blooming.

Soft is a morning rain
falling in the Garden
nurturing all living things,
bathing them in delicate showers
whose pitter-pat
promises fresh greenery
and sparkling colors
from myriad blooms
who love to have their
faces washed.

Easy are golden-pink sunbeams
peaking through
congenial clouds,
inviting a little group
of white-tail deer
to venture from

their hidden shelter
into a cool oak grove
carpeted in sweet clover—
their favorite meal
for peaceful munching.

A mother deer looks up
from feeding,
then two and more
until they all are staring
straight into my eyes—
not in fear or apprehension
but in trust and curiosity
(for I am yet a stranger here)
in perfect calm
and such fearlessness
as is startling to me.

An irony, indeed,
for how often have I
startled such as these
while rushing
through their forest homes.

Here in the Garden's safe repose
gentle herbivores
need not scamper away

and so they stand
as if in meditation
and conscious intention
that I should absorb
the depth of
their gentle essence.

And as I gaze into
their moist, dark chocolate eyes
a deep communion
flows between us
while all my questions
melt away
in their confidence
that seems to say:

We know that we are cherished here.
So may you also understand
and thrive in Garden harmony.
Now go lightly on your journey
as we enjoy this heavenly clover.

They lower their heads
as if to say, *Grace*,
and I arise to walk on,
treading softly.

Dolphin Medicine

Speak to me of Nature's rhythms!
O, ancient ones who follow sailors
For safekeeping, sounding warning
Rescuing those who've lost their way
In the darkness of deep waters.

At my call, Dolphin emerges
Spinning spirals through the ocean
Communing with Great Spirit's essence
As keeper of the sacred breath
That regenerates all life,
As above and so below
The surface of our consciousness.

Unbeknownst to many pilgrims
On a far side of the Garden
Exists a vast teal-blue lagoon
Where creatures from every dimension
Thrive and play in liquid radiance
Unburdened by mankind's detritus

For these are crystal healing waters
Reserved for elemental life
To be restored, just as we humans
Have our own transforming fountain.

Here is mighty Dolphin's realm
Where he speaks all languages
And understands the vital need

Of creating loving-kindness,
For life is rough on Planet Earth.

Whales and dolphins take their turn
At basking in the clear lagoon
While charging it with energy
Garnered from the depths they dive
Out in the Garden's wildest seas
That hold a balance for our Earth
Until we choose to be enlightened.

I now attend with alert mind—
For of all the animal guides
Dolphin speaks most lucidly
Through body, mind, and spirit channels
As mediator between species
And Gaia's advocate for oneness.

O, how my soul longs to reach out—
To join in Dolphin's happy play
Diving down among bright fishes
Flipping my tail to rise up
As if standing on the water
Laughing, splashing with my fellows

Urging humans to understand
The ocean is the womb of Earth.
This Garden holds its clear reflection
Where souls are born, and born again
To bring our planet safely Home.

"But first you must become like me,"
A spinner dolphin telepaths.

"*Cetacea** breathing is the key
You need to dispel energies
And burdens of anxiety.

Just breathe in deep and gently hold
As long as you can safely do—
Until your heart begins to race,
Then blow out with a solid *puh!*
And feel your troubled mind release.

Now breathe again and follow me
Beneath the waves of our lagoon."

Instantly I find myself
In an oceanic realm
Swimming with my dolphin pod
Who seem to know me as their own

Perhaps as an adopted calf
In need of their particular gifts
Of telepathic sonar rays
That spiral straight into my being—
Body, soul and mind and heart,
Until I feel dense blockages
Evaporate in one great *whoosh!*

*Biological order of whales and dolphins

While the dolphins dance and play
Vivaciously around my head.

As together we ascend
Back up to the airy surface,
I notice that my fins are gone
And I am once again on shore

Now with a renewed life force
Surging through my consciousness
My entire psyche filled with peace
And vigor that is Garden-born.

Then the dolphins speak again:

> "Learn to spiral in this flow
> And return often to our realm
> Back into the ocean's womb.
>
> Then carry knowledge out to those
> Who need our equanimity,
> For we would see all humans healed
> And Earth made whole eternally.
>
> Please take our message to your kind
> So they will happily embrace
> The power of this medicine
> We fervently desire to share.

Balancing

In the Garden
lives a man who balances rocks
anywhere

Creating inspired formations
in fields, streams, beaches—
anywhere

He finds the breathless still point
that can withstand strong winds
anywhere

The rock tells him—it's not just
anywhere

But a particular place or plane set
anywhere

Upon the perfectly matching face
of its harmonious mate
with which it could stay forever
anywhere

Love could be like that—
balancing.

At Peace Amongst the Pines

Each pine forest is a renewal grove
A healer lives in every tree
Beneath whose boughs the fairies dance

For pine aroma purifies
Rejuvenating those who breathe
The healing incense of needle and bark
Whose essence calms body and mind
Even for the fairy folk.

Pines are sentinels of peace
Watchmen on the wall of Life
Holding a vision of harmony
As ancient guardians of the land
Of sea and sky and all who live
And travel through their sylvan homes.

Evergreens mark a well-trod path
Between the Here and Over There
Safe harbor for adventurers
Who stop a while midst their sojourns

To be comforted by healing balms
To rise beyond their current state
To lift up high as pine trees do
And keep on reaching for the stars.

Expand the Circle of Perception

*Once touched
by Love's immensity,
your world will never
be the same.*

A Symphony of Light and Shadow

Here in the Garden
You will find what you bring
And more if you desire,
As numinous creatures and landscapes
Reveal profound realities.

Earth and water, stone and flower
All flow together in perfect harmony—
A symphony of light and shadow
That rises and falls
Under dramatic skies

Reflecting what you wish to release
And offering what longs to be embraced
As simplicity and the plain holiness
Of peace that comes in leaving behind
What no longer holds you back.

In the Velvet

Have you ever kissed a horse's nose,
Nuzzled a fluffy baby duck,
Or felt an otter's luxurious fur—
Stroked a kitten's silky back,
Or allowed a single fingertip
To caress the petal of a rose?

Each one is velvety to the touch,
Exquisite in its downy power
To cause the heart to sigh and ache
With deepest longing to become
An organ of compassion's fire
And tender transformation.

Reclining in a fragrant bower,
I'm enfolded in such tenderness
That suddenly I'm like a babe
Who has discovered only now
The ecstasy of owning toes

As I leap up and sweep around
The Garden in communion with
Softness's euphoric delight
Filling my heightened senses with
The sweet rapture of velvet's skill
In opening my yearning heart
And healing it of brittleness.

Imagine being delicately enfolded
By an etheric atmosphere
That's silky soft as cashmere mittens.

Such is my experience,
When silently an exquisite angel
Emerges from her lilied seat,
Arrayed in iridescent colors
Jewel-toned like hummingbird wings.

She smiles kindly as I rub my cheek
Against a tiny red fox kit,
And conveys to me an inspiring notion:

> "Your own sweet soul is just as soft.
> Did you know we hug you, too,
> In the shelter of Spirit's world
> When your hardened shells come off
> Because it's safe to be exposed.
>
> You will notice that your guides
> Move about like butterflies
> Wafting on a summer breeze;
> For Nature's tactile purity
> Is both reminder and reflection
> Of the soul's finest character.

"Here's a secret you'll not hear
Outside the sphere of Gaia's Home:

*The swiftest path to soul freedom
Is to cultivate its tenderness.
Become receptive to Spirit's touch
And a universe of loveliness
Will gladly gather at your feet.*

See how you already shimmer
In the midst of new-found friends,
So many plants and animals
Just waiting for your light caress.

Don't be surprised if you discover
Fairies napping on your shoulder;
They are particularly fond
Of humans who are waking up."

And so it is in Gaia's Garden,
I muse, remembering the Snow Angel—
Then notice that her gift is glowing
As if the wrapping were transparent.

Power Meets Power

While exploring Garden mysteries
I've discovered myriad healing sites
Where groups and individuals
Commune with the elements
Of earth and water, air and fire
Learning lessons of soul growth
And stretching their own consciousness.

At the beach I come upon
A robust man out in the ocean,
Open to the random waves
The swirling fronds of sea kelp
Or a sudden breaker catching him
Oftentimes by surprise.

Even the threat of toppling over
Does not appear to phase him.
In fact, he seems to court some danger
As he ventures beyond the confluence
Of roiling sea and glistening sand
Offering his body to the tide
That washes briskly all around him
Without opinion or resistance.

Eventually, I return by an unknown path
That leads me unexpectedly
To meet him as he climbs up
From a wind-swept sand dune.

"You and the surf appear to be
In a dynamic conversation,"
I comment, risking an intrusion.

"Yes," he smiles in quick response.

"I frequently visit this boundless shore
To remember what true power is
Instead of what I'm expected to wield
As head of the large companies
That often are my chosen work.

I expand my gaze to the vast horizon
Then walk into the rising tide
To feel this ocean's mighty force
Of cosmic eternality
In contrast to earth-life's short span.

So I go back to mortal realms
As a much humbler fellow—
A simple guy with sandy feet
And salt air in my nostrils."

I thank him as he waves, *Good-bye*
And make a promise to myself
To take my shoes off back on Earth
And dare to get my own feet wet.

Eagle Views

High up in his Garden aerie
sits the Majestic Bald Eagle

Symbol of Great Spirit

Master of Soul Freedom

Conqueror of Fear

Dweller in the Heaven World

Keen of Insight and Perception

Emblem of a State of Grace
Achieved Through Initiation

Those who venture to Eagle's realm
Follow the passion of their hearts
Welcome the Unknown's enigma
Surrender to Great Mystery's path
Summon Wisdom's deep courage
Fly in faith toward the sun.

Mighty Eagle beckons me:

> "Rise up now and spread your wings.
> Trust the wind to carry us aloft
> As we survey what you have not seen
> About your own reality."

As we fly high up in the Garden,
Clouds soon obscure it from our view
Till there is nothing left to see
Except the sun and bright blue sky.

We stretch our wings for altitude
Then catch a current as we climb
Rising on the warming thermals
Spiraling in glorious loops
Then banking eastward in a turn.

Perching deftly on a cloud—
(Which we birds do in Gaia's realm)
Eagle lands and bids me rest.

> "We'll stop here, fold in your wings.
> Sit next to me, for I desire
> To infuse your hungry mind
> With the wisdom Eagle bears.
>
> More than any other gift
> Mankind has desired to fly
> To break the tethers of gravity
> And soar with eagles to the sun
> In our celestial convocations
>
> To reach up high for new perspectives
> Courage, strength, and understanding

"Of the visions given to those
Who push the limits of self-discovery
While seeking Spirit's beauty and grace.

Consider what you felt just now
As you flew on rapturous wings.
Anchor that experience
Firmly in your consciousness
For its memory will expand
Your capacity for higher thought,
And increased receptivity
To intimations from our realm."

Observing now my eagle-self
I feel precision of eye sight
To view the landscape's tapestry
While noticing a salmon's splash.

My beak is sharp and powerful
A piercing cry sounds in my throat
As lungs breathe in the rarefied air—
Exhilarating, crisp and clear.

I feel my body sleek and smooth
My wings enormous in their span.
Talons keen formed on strong feet
Made for grasping when I hunt.

To be an eagle honors me
To sense such grand nobility.
No wonder native shamans esteem
Eagle Medicine above all others.

His golden-eyed gaze upon me says:

> "Go deeper now into your center
> And find the nature of the soul
> Reflected in your eagle-self.
> Reach within to learn the truth."

Yes, meditating makes all clear:
I feel my higher mind's insight
Of how to be more like this one—
The chief among all winged creatures.

Eagle is impeccable.
Unfettered in his soaring flight
Connected to the heaven world
And yet at home on earthly planes
With Mother Earth and Father Sky.

Assuringly, he nods assent:

> "So are you also meant to rise
> As co-creator with Great Spirit,
> Tender steward of the Earth

"Wayfarer upon the bridge
That links the Here and Over There
And welcome visitor in Gaia's realm.

This is the truth that you have sought.
Accept no limits on your flight
Embrace a Garden state of mind
Expand the circle of your vision.

Now that you've shared in Eagle's view
I trust you'll reach up for the heights
Nothing less will satisfy
Your thirst for freedom of the skies."

Lifting off his misty perch,
His snowy head glistening in the sun,
Eagle bids me to the air
For one last flight on raptor wings
That leaves me, flightless, by a lake
Where I can watch my noble friend
Ascend in his magnificence.

And then I find an eagle feather—
Never given casually,
Usually earned through Spirit's tests,
Tied onto Snow Angel's gift.

A Sylphic Serenade

Soundless as air, ever-present as mind,
A thousand pairs of slender sylphs
Elegantly grace the azure sky
In wispy cirrus-cloud formation

Tenderly wafting on the gentle breeze
Then flying with the four winds
To other Garden corners and back again
Whooshing! invisibly around me
Seamlessly communicating
Devotion to their sacred purpose:

> We sylphs dance together
> like a *pas de deux*
> of twin souls
> in perfect harmony,
> weaving currents
> of Spirit Mind
> through the Garden
> to your world.
>
> We move in
> balanced synchrony
> as male and female
> intertwine
> as day and night
> become each other

      as separation
      loses meaning

      and paradox
      is resolved
      within
      the awakened mind

      that understands
      all things to be
      both more and less
      than they usually appear.

Are the sylphs truly speaking to me—
Or am I only hearing wind
Rustling through trees
Or murmuring amongst tall grasses?

Yes! My heart confirms:

This is an ethereal transmission
Becoming a whispered serenade—
An exhilarating wind-in-my-face sense
Of being more than I thought I could be.

And I swear I hear sylphs singing:

"Mystic forces gather here,
sylphs come 'round from far and near.

Gaia calls us to her bower
the breath of life on all to shower.

We who are of mind and air
permeate the Garden fair

balancing both left and right
as the day goes with the night.

Masculine and feminine
hand in glove are joined as one

for we would see all souls go free
to live as happy as do we.

Purity is our domain
the trackless realms of air we claim

to help all beings amplify
and raise their sights up to the sky.

Here in the Garden we transform
the thoughts of those who arrive forlorn

"into calming waves of peace
leading their heart-minds to release

limitations, doubts, or fears
that may have burdened them for years.

Sylphs fly unfettered everywhere
making merry without care

with angels of the living flame
who join us in our special game

of telepathing mind to mind
the thoughts of creatures loving and kind

so that unity prevails
throughout the Garden without fail.

For Spirit Mind can know no bounds
so heart connections must be found.

We create them by our skill
in gathering faithful souls who will

to love each other in purely sharing
a *t'ai chi* dance of impeccable caring.

"Sylphs are essential to all life,
even here without the strife

of earthly ills or human woes
our sacred fire breath always flows.

For we are part of all domains
our Presence helps ensure the gains

expanding insight offers all
who strive for good, answering the call

to walk the path of Spirit's way
to seek the radiance of day

the Divine Mind to manifest
and know the peace of perfect rest.

Sylphs are jubilant in flight
we breathe out bliss with all our might

to keep the Garden atmosphere
charged with loving-kindness here

to cultivate a consciousness
that uplifts all without duress.

"We carry Gaia's Love abroad
to all who walk the Good Red Road

as shamans call Life's rigorous course
that leads the soul back to its Source.

Our task is to expand the view
of many eyes, not just the few.

Sylph magnetism we employ
to raise all up in boundless joy

for we would set all life forms free—
come to the Garden,
your True Self to be."

The Ascent

"Come join me up here!"

A cheerful voice seems to
Emanate from a small cloud
Hugging the hillside till it dissolves
Revealing my dear Ah-Lahn
Perched upon a rocky shelf
Overlooking the landscape.

> "I want you to expand your view
> Of what is possible in life.
> For limitations must drop away
> Before you can fulfill the task
> That Mother Gaia asked of you."

Ascending the Garden's steep inclines
Is easy as a dream time thought.
I will my way to Ah-Lahn's side
And so begins a profound lesson—
An experience I'll never forget.

> "Look out now; breathe in the sights."

He gently turns me 'round to see
A luxuriant valley spread out below
Lushly green, fertile with fields
Of lavender and daffodils,
Tulips and blossoming fruit trees
Tinting the air with new life's scents
As springtime touches Paradise.

Inhaling deep, I feel a tingle
Moving up and down my spine
Coming to rest behind my heart
Where Ah-Lahn has placed his hand.

    "Let us move on, there's more to see."

He beckons me to walk this time
As humans do on our two feet
To feel the solid ground beneath
To breathe a mountain's crisp, clear air
To feel the sun warm on my back

And marvel as the mountain top
Seems to recede as further up
We climb an ever-steepening slope
Where Ah-Lahn sees my perplexed look.

    "There's always higher to attain.
      Don't worry now, we are nearly there.
      See—look again, expand your gaze."

The valley has appeared to shrink
With fields and trees now color spots
And in the distance a great sea
That seems to wrap the Garden 'round.

Standing there in rapturous gaze
I feel my consciousness expand
As if I could contain this world

By simply breathing in the view,
Even as I also feel
A reciprocating breath
As if the world inhales me too
Like sweethearts who pour out
Their deep affection to each other.

Placing his hand upon my brow
Ah-Lahn brings me back to him
And softly whispers in my ear:

> "We've more ascent to make today."

Then holding me about the waist
He lifts us up from where we stand
Flying aloft through wispy clouds
Until we reach what appears to be
The highest Himalayan peak

The very center of this world
Whose breadth spreads out directionless
With every view consisting of
Both the Here and Over There.

Even more amazing still
Above us hangs a Firmament
Shaped dome-like, enfolding all
Bright with stars and yet not dark
Perfectly illumined as it is
By a glow not single-sourced

That bathes the scene in purity
Transforming all into itself

Revealing sweet Ah-Lahn and me
As orbs of luminous stardust
That telepaths in clearest thought:

> *This is what you really are—*
> *A radiant beam from God's own heart*
> *A soul of Light magnificent*
> *Sent to Earth to bless and heal*
> *Then to return as your Real Self*
> *That you discover on the path*
> *You walk in faith and charity.*

Then Ah-Lahn whispers once more:

> "Now I must take you back, my dear,
> To where your Garden trek moves on
> Yet with a wider view of life
> And encouragement to persevere.
>
> For you now see the Otherworld;
> It is your Home, as well as mine
> Where one day we'll unite in Love
> And stray no more in worlds of time."

Garden Traces

Like delicate golden flower pollen
    dusting a bee's wings,
    I know that traces of the Garden
    will linger in my consciousness,
    even when I've wandered
    back to earthly climes.

Now I know myself as more
    than who I thought I'd ever be—
    for who could hope to stay the same
    after dancing with fiery elementals,
    meeting gracious Mother Gaia
    and profoundly communing with
    a living, breathing Paradise.

Etched into the crystal chalice
    of my soul's reality
    these experiences leave behind
    an outline of their quintessence—
    and blessing of sweet unity
    that offers deeper knowledge of
    my purpose and identity.

Walking in the Garden today
    I feel a lightness in my step,
    notice how my heart now burns
    in gratitude for being alive

and I rejoice in new-found compassion
for those souls who have forgot
the Otherworld is very real.

As this numinous path unfolds
    I have hope that with a gentle touch
    a kind word or sincere smile

    I may yet impart to Life
    a slight taste of fairy magic
    or a hint of fragrant rose

    that will tarry in my aura
    each time that I travel outward
    from the precious journey inward

    to the sanctuary of my heart
    that is the Garden and the Home
    of my soul's own dear beloved.

Feel the Heartbeat of Mother Earth

*Life is different here
in the Garden of true being
because Spirit has revealed
your innermost reality.*

Gentle Steps

The Garden teaches lessons wise,
most notably is how to be
when one traverses holy ground.

walk softly in this place
so the footprints you leave
may be tracks of Light

walk softly in this place
lest you disturb the peace
of Nature's breath
as she takes in human suffering
exhaling healing transformation

walk softly in this place
so all your words
may disappear into a vision
of oneness with the life of things
that only can be known
when gentle steps
become the habit
of your being here

The Grand

To hear the heartbeat
>of the Garden's grandest peak
>one must step away
>and sit by a lake on a still day
>and listen to waves on rocks,
>to the flutter of aspen leaves

And then to the deep breath
>of awareness as it gently ventures
>into water so clear that
>only its emerald-blue reflection
>gives it away.

Then, and only then,
>in the silence
>>of Nature's fluid present
>>a vibration arises.

Like the pulsing tone
>of eight bass violins,
>your body feels it
>before your ears notice.

This is the sound
>the Grand makes
>sitting in perpetual majesty,
>a source of power,
>illumination and peace.

The Source your soul longs for,
    the beacon that has
    drawn you to itself
    over the crystal cord
    of loving-kindness
    that has ever connected
    you to the summit of reality

Forever and always here.

Communion

Water gently burbling
on pink rocks
intense, hot, golden sun
beating on my skin
warm and nourishing.

I feed on the heat
and drink in the glow
of subtle golds and browns
reds and greens
a touch of violet

and shafts of willow fingers
reaching for a brilliant, cloudless
ceiling so blue
my heart cannot contain
its purity or seamlessness.

The sky just is—
resting its gentle presence
on the mountaintops,
it stays and stays
not moving, ever here

as each of my senses opens
to this Garden realm
where seen and unseen meet
in the very center of my heart.

Relishing the moment
I inhale the breeze
as loquacious pine trees
beckon me into a misty grove
to share a mutual embrace

with my head upon
one sylvan breast
whose mossy bark
soothes my cheek
inviting me to press in close
that I might detect her
whispered history
held in ancient rings
of faithful growth.

I sense the movement
of rich sap urging
branches to reach up high
and roots to grow down deep
anchoring the landscape
and the sky
together in profound
communion

all in the present,
ever-changing now
that is true sanctuary.

Eternity lives in this place—
in water, rock, and tree
in tiny ant that crawls
upon a twig,
in spiky seed
or crunching gravel
underfoot,
in bird that flies
a Spirit course.

I have come home to a place
long held in my heart
and that has held me
as a mother cradles her young.

O, magnificent is this Luminosity
who deftly employs her loving-kindness
as a mirror that reveals to me
the new Self I am birthing.

I am becoming the Mother
I have always wanted,
and this Garden enfolds me
as one of her own.

Bright as Diamonds, Pure as Gold

In the midst of mountain gazing
Imagining the hall of an alpine king
Suddenly I'm underground
Next to a group of stalwart gnomes
Working in a vein of gold.

I immediately apologize:
"Please excuse my dropping in."

> "Oh, it happens all the time,"
> Answers a gnome in mining gear,
> His sonorous voice both deep and rich.

> "All the elements like to play
> Especially with visitors.
> My name is Myron, by the way.
> Would you enjoy a workshop tour?"

"Oh, yes! I've never been good at physical things.
I'm curious to see how you gnomes work."

> "This is one of our best sites
> For producing crystals of clear quartz.
> You'll notice that we grow them here."

Incredibly, I see it's true—
Crystals expanding before my eyes
As an army of gnomes in white coveralls
Lays tiny translucent building blocks
So the facets grow equally.

"How do you fashion such perfection?
What are the ingredients?"

> "It all depends on what we're making
> And the colors that we want.
> Clear quartz is mostly sand and air
> So we make a lot of it.
>
> For diamonds we use pure stardust
> And powerful energy wielded by
> Experts with a surgeon's touch.
>
> We love to work with hands and tools
> To fashion gemstone artistry
> So master craftsmen also create
> Exquisite jewels as focuses
> Of elevated consciousness
> For use by guides and their elders
> In ceremonies and sacred rites.
>
> But they prefer to come to us
> To meditate in gemstone rooms
> We open up as Light retreats
> For energetic balancing
> Within this dimension and beyond.
>
> Come down this hall, and I'll show you.
> Experience is worth a thousand words."

A long corridor stretches before us
The full length of a football field
With gem-lined chambers on either side
Each one designed to anchor solely
A single mineral's energy.

We enter an alcove of amethyst.
Its frequency of sweet forgiveness
Makes me sigh euphorically,
"O, this is the *nicest* place."

> "I know," says Myron, with a smile.
>
> "Flower devas adore this spot
>   It lifts them up and makes them glad
>   To bloom wherever Gaia plants them.
>
> Please step into our emerald room;
> We love its cave-like intensity.
> The Green Man and I visit here.
> He soaks up intense healing rays
> With which to permeate the Garden.
> I come here as gnome supervisor
> To clear my vision for our best work.
>
> Some of the chambers are occupied
> So I can't show them all to you
> But I think you'll like blue chalcedony
> For its balancing vibration."

Immediately I feel the energy
Of patience, trust, and divine will
Spread through my auric field
As elevated thought and speech.

"What about the ruby room?"
I ask as Myron passes it by.

> "Only high adepts go in there.
> No one else can bear its power
> As a focus of pure Love—
> The essence of Divinity.
> We do not know its origin,
> But we all hold it in profound regard.
>
> And now I have a treat for you."

With his blue eyes all a-twinkle,
Myron escorts me to a vaulted space
That contains a translucent chair
Made of coalesced starlight
Its back and sides inlaid with gems—
All faceted in sheer perfection.

> "This is our atomic accelerator,
> Great masters come here for renewal
> After working with your world.
> One day you may sit here too.
> I think you'll get a charge from it!"

Myron laughs at his own jokes
And has been dancing through our tour
While other gnomes sing happy tunes
That seem to activate all matter.

Soil and stone and wood obey them
Molding easily into new forms
Almost in response to thought
And definitely to the energy
I see and feel them focusing
On the structures that they build.

This is a song I hear them sing:

> *O work and play*
> *Are both the same,*
> *They're fun for us*
> *By any name.*
>
> *Molding matter*
> *Into form*
> *Brings joy and laughter*
> *To us gnomes.*
>
> *We're faithful, strong*
> *Courageous, too,*
> *Creative, smart*
> *And loyal to*
> *Sweet Gaia's plan*
> *For Garden life.*

> *We hold the balance*
> *Without strife,*
> *For matter follows*
> *Our command*
> *So we can build*
> *This crystal land.*
>
> *We'll work and play*
> *Until the end,*
> *Calling all we meet*
> *Partner and friend.*

After such a rousing song
I cannot help but clap with glee
As Myron earnestly goes on:

> "Humans don't take us seriously.
> In point of fact, we create the ground
> That holds this etheric plane together.
>
> We are closest in vibration
> To the dimension where you live
> So we understand your needs
> And relish taking care of you.
>
> We're also the Garden's alchemists
> Turning sunlight into gold
> Anchoring its purity
> For Gaia's realm and for your own."

We enter now a glistening hallway
Lined with crystals of gigantic size
Flashing beams of diamond brilliance
Between veins of purest gold—
Yes, it shines bright as the sun.

I see a gnome in a side room,
Obviously not to be disturbed,
Staring intently at a plain white wall
Of milky stone without facets.

> "Oh, that's our senior crystal designer
> His creativity knows no bounds.
> He's making up a brand new form
> To surprise Gaia when she visits."

Next are woodshops filled with carvers
Artisans of enormous skill
Working walnut, cherry, and oak
Into fantastical designs

Of spiral stairways, clocks, and furniture
Interiors for Garden abodes
Inhabited by residents who find comfort
In their masterfully gnome-made homes.

Then we meet miners happily scooping
Shovels full of mineral-rich ore
Into carts sent to the jewelers
For their gorgeous gem creations.

And finally we approach a granite wall
Where a hundred gnomes work side by side
Laughing and joking with each other
Doing what looks like finger painting

Creating swirls of pink and black
Embedded with tiny golden crystals
Swooping patterns that penetrate
Hundreds of feet into the mountain.

"O, that looks like so much fun!"

I can hardly contain myself
In the presence of such beauty
And powerful energetic vibration
Emanating from the graceful stones.

> "It is, and these are coveted positions
> Only held by our best artists.
> Novices can cause such a mess!
>
> One of them made an entire mountain
> Appear as if it had the measles.
> That required some serious clean-up."
>
> He smiles and chuckles to himself—
> "I think we changed it to obsidian."

I wish that I could stay much longer
The gnomes hold secrets I long to learn.

But Myron says the tour is over
At least for now, though I may return.
Then he adds kindly with a spritely jig:

> "As you make your way through life
> Remember this advice from gnomes:
>
> *The more grounded you become*
> *The higher up your soul can climb.*
>
> And don't forget, you're also made
> Out of stardust and sunlight—
> Bright as diamonds, pure as gold."

Enough

It does not matter
where I am
in the sanctuary
of the heart
for here am I
in my wholeness.

An amazing contemplation:
to feel sufficient
in the moment,
to be in ecstasy
with living

To feel
a natural openness
embracing what arises
on my journey
through this Place Beyond.

We cannot predict
to what or whom
we will be called.

When life is an adventure
and Spirit the guide,
anything can happen
and usually does.

The sun rises pink and fiery
over the mountains
that greet this morning
in confidence.

Their solid majesty
affirms
that in
this blessed place

Spirit is alive in me,
and that is
quite enough.

Fly into the Arms of Reunion

We are dwellers on two planets
and no one is the wiser
except we two
whose silent ships
sail joyfully amongst the stars.

Gaia's Blessing

May our Home always be the sanctuary
to which you return
after every earthly sojourn.

May you carry a Garden frame of mind
and heart to any world
that calls to you.

May you cherish all living things
as elements of your True Self.

May you always know the peace
of ineffable Love and Joy
that are the Garden's pure delights
and gifts of perfect healing for all time.

May you feel the gratitude
of spirit beings and earthly ones
who recognize there is a bridge
between the Here and Over There.

And may you live to see the day
when the veil between our worlds
dissolves.

The Green Man's Comfort

A powerful intuition startles me:

My Garden journey draws to a close.
The thought of leaving makes me cry.
I've got to talk to the Green Man—
The one my elemental friends call, Uncle.
He will know what I should do.

Hurrying to the entrance gate
I find him conversing with an elf
Who graciously bows and glides away
As Uncle embraces me with a smile.

> "Hello, my dear, how may I help?
> You're looking very bright these days.
> But what are those worries on your brow?"

I cannot stop the tears that come
As I pour out my heart to him:

"O, Uncle, I don't want to leave this place,
But Mother Gaia gave her blessing.
Is she, then, dismissing me?
Have I answered her request?"

> "O, Gaia's gratitude runs deep
> For the insights you have gained
> Through your adventures in her realm.

"And, yes, you have fulfilled her tasks
Save one—that I will tell you now,
For it concerns your guide, Ah-Lahn.

The future of your mutual bond
Depends upon your willingness
To completely resolve past hurts
The two of you have caused each other.

He yearns to welcome you for good
Into the sanctuary of his heart—
Which is safe harbor for your soul,
Even as your higher consciousness
Holds the key to his ascent.

Here is what we ask of you:

> *Can you sustain a resonance*
> *With us here in Gaia's realm*
> *To work in faithful harmony*
> *With the one who knows you best?*

If you agree, then go to him,
Affirm your love and commitment.
Our Garden waits upon your choice
That portends blessings for us all."

"O, thank you, Uncle, you've eased my mind!
Of course, I'll do what you request.
To know that I may help my guide
Is a blessing to my life.

I could hug you here forever!
But now I must be on my way.
I cannot wait to tell Ah-Lahn
We still have Garden tasks to share!"

Reunion

Before Uncle gives me leave to go
To begin my journey's next phase
He bids me sit beneath an oak
And listen while he reveals
A deeper purpose of my mission
And what true reunion means.

Here are Uncle's words to me:

> "Releasing fear of the other
> Allows mutual resonance
> To arise in hearts
> Who once were close
> But drifted apart
> In turbulent waters.
>
> What or whom
> Have you feared
> To embrace?
>
> Learn that story,
> See yourself as that hero.
>
> Revive compassion
> For those struggles,
> And forgive the chasm
> That opened
> Between you.

"Only loving-kindness
 Can build a bridge
 Twixt self and other
 Creating unity of mind and heart.

In truth,
You have walked
Together for eons—
Though you knew it not.

Understand this as
The Garden's greatest gift
Which you once knew
And now must learn again:

> *All of Life is one*
> *With all of Life,*
> *And reunion marks*
> *The dissolution*
> *Of fragmentation*
> *So wholeness may prevail.*

Go be fearless
And feel Unity resounding
In every corner of your psyche.

That is how you may remain
In the Garden that you adore."

Opening the Gift

Referring to the precious box
That I have carried faithfully
Throughout this profound adventure,
Ah-Lahn fixes me with a serious eye.

> "Have you guessed the contents
> Of the Snow Angel's special gift?
> I trust you have not broken the seal."

A smile flickers about his lips
As I forthrightly answer him:

"I am no curious Pandora
And I would not tempt the Fates
By opening this gift too soon.
The Snow Angel said that I should wait
Until I'd been here for a while.

I am puzzled, though, Ah-Lahn—
Every so often I have felt
A new element being added
Giving the box more substance
Yet simultaneously less weight."

> "Why do you suppose that's so?"

"You spoke of spiritual gravity—
  The force of Light that pulls me higher

"To elude Earth's limitations
   To aim my soul's eye on the stars.

In your Presence, dear Ah-Lahn,
I've come to know that force as Love.
So I believe that is my gift—
The one the Snow Angel said
That I would offer to myself,
The one you've surely given me."

He nods his gracious assent.
No other urging is required
For me to risk with trembling hands
To untie the bright green bow
Remove red wrapping from the box
And cautiously peer deep inside
To find...the plainest of hand mirrors!

"Oh, no!" I gasp, "How can this be!
I was so sure I felt the gift.
Was this journey all in vain?
Have I disappointed you?"

> "No, my darling, you perceived aright.
> The gift is Love and much, much more,
> Though not as you imagined it.
> Now take the mirror and look within;
> Tell me what it shows to you."

"I see my own reflection here,
Yet not as I have ever been.
Such radiance astonishes me.
Have I begun to glow like you?"

    "Of course, my dear, and now go deeper.
      Is yours the only image you see?"

He places his hand upon my brow
And suddenly the mirror grows
Enveloping me in the scene
Of the Garden's cosmic vastness
Where every creature wears my face
As if we were one and the same.

As I stand transfixed and awed
Unable to ask why or how
The Garden glows with incandescence
Infusing me with unspeakable joy

A feeling of immeasurable unity
That fills my heart and mind and soul
With a luminous sense of deep kinship
For every kind of living thing.

Sweet Gaia's Home is enfolding me
Even as I contain it all.

My dear guide bids me look once more
While touching my brow most tenderly.

So as the Garden fades from view
I peer into the mirror's depth
And see *his* face reflected back
As if it were my very own.
And then I hear him speak to me:

> "I am your gift, as you are mine,
> Your faithful work has made it so.
> And thus, my darling, you have earned
> Your place beside me for all time
> Even as you journey on
> Back and forth across the bridge
> Between your earthly home and here
> Until your labor is complete."

"O, dear Ah-Lahn, my heart is full!
My rapture cannot be described
Except to say, embued with Love
And in its all-pervading bliss
I realize my heart and yours
Have been transformed here in the Garden.
United for Eternity
In Spirit's fire and pure delight—
Reunion's promise fulfilled at last."

When Two Become One

No one can predict
when sweethearts will converge
when those who were two
will suddenly merge.

Both male and female
concentric at last—
nested adoringly
where separation is past.

He enfolds She
as the Spirit the Earth,
and She blesses He
with her soul's strong rebirth.

So begins a fresh cycle
with new moon's release
of Love's perfect promise
rooted in peace.

For harmony reigns
when two souls such as these
take flight as their future
wafts in on the breeze

of Spirit's *Purusha!*
as its out-breath is called,
that lifts them in holiness
no longer to fall.

Their journey was arduous,
though not without joy,
to accomplish this union
of a girl and a boy

who found strength in losing
each other to death
that never deterred them
from destiny's depth.

As pilgrims through time
they trusted the path
to carry them forward
from life until life

so they might one day
stand united in bliss
all radiant, resplendent
receiving a kiss

from devoted angels
who merrily share
in sweet celebration
with those who most care

that this man and this woman
should strive to become
a glad manifestation
of Love's Victory won.

Acknowledgements

I have heard it said that gratitude opens the way to all other blessings. Life has proved to me the truth of that statement many times over.

I know of several people who create gratitude journals as a practice that keeps them in that attitude—to maintain the open heart and mind that gratitude nurtures.

For me, writing poetry has the same effect of opening my heart and mind to a flow of enlightening experience.

The poetical atmosphere is a mystical space, a realm of consciousness to which I find myself homing. The opportunity to visit that place and live there for periods of time is a grace for which I am eternally grateful.

The muse is a marvelous aspect of being. I do not pretend to fully understand her or him. Inspiration appears in a number of guises. And isn't that part of the beautiful mystery that has for centuries beckoned poets to brave the Unknown in hopes of coming out the other side with a few lines that may delight or inspire or even heal.

Such is my experience and a profound reason for the gratitude I am offering here along with profound thanks to my colleagues Theresa McNicholas, James Bennett, and Paula Kehoe, and to the artists whose public domain images we have chosen for this volume.

May you, dear reader, feel my gratitude flow from these verses. Writing them has been a gift that I am joyfully grateful to share.

A Poet of Soul & Fire

Cheryl Lafferty Eckl is a mystical poetess and storyteller who writes in the ecstatic tradition of Rumi and Hafiz.

She lives in Livingston, Montana, where she finds profound inspiration in the surrounding mountains, rivers, lakes, and Big Sky spaces that have long been recognized as places of spiritual connection and healing.

An award-winning author of multiple books, Cheryl continues to embrace life's myriad transitions as she writes, teaches, and pays deep attention to the poetics of her soul.

To learn more about her work, please visit her website at www.CherylEckl.com.

www.ingramcontent.com/pod-product-compliance
Lightning Source LLC
Chambersburg PA
CBHW021128300426
44113CB00006B/339